Who Are You, Lord?

Raeann Fitz

WHO ARE YOU, LORD?
By Raeann Fitz
Published by Creation House Press
A Strang Company
600 Rinehart Road
Lake Mary, Florida 32746
www.creationhouse.com

This book or parts thereof may not be reproduced in any form, stored in a retrieval system or transmitted in any form by any means—electronic, mechanical, photocopy, recording or otherwise—without prior written permission of the publisher, except as provided by United States of America copyright law.

Unless otherwise noted, all Scripture quotations are from the Amplified Bible. Old Testament copyright © 1965, 1987 by the Zondervan Corporation. The Amplified New Testament copyright © 1954, 1958, 1987 by the Lockman Foundation. Used by permission.

Scripture quotations marked RSV are from the Revised Standard Version of the Bible. Copyright © 1946, 1952, 1971 by the Division of Christian Education of the National Council of the Churches of Christ in the USA. Used by permission.

Scripture quotations marked NKJV are from the New King James Version of the Bible. Copyright © 1979, 1980, 1982 by Thomas Nelson, Inc., publishers. Used by permission.

Scripture quotations marked NASB are from the New American Standard Bible. Copyright © 1960, 1962, 1963, 1968, 1971, 1972, 1973, 1975, 1977, 1995 by the Lockman Foundation. Used by permission. (www.Lockman.org)

Scripture quotations marked NRSV are from the New Revised Standard Version of the Bible. Copyright © 1989 by the Division of Christian Education of the National Council of the Churches of Christ in the USA. Used by permission.

Scripture quotations marked NIV are from the Holy Bible, New International Version. Copyright © 1973, 1978, 1984, International Bible Society. Used by permission.

Scripture quotations marked KJV are from the King James Version of the Bible.

Scripture quotations marked NLT are from the Holy Bible, New Living Translation, copyright © 1996. Used by permission of Tyndale House Publishers, Inc., Wheaton, IL 60189. All rights reserved.

Cover design by Terry Clifton
Interior design by David Bilby

Copyright © 2004 by Raeann Fitz
All rights reserved

Library of Congress Control Number: 2004102754
International Standard Book Number: 1-59185-561-6

04 05 06 07 08 — 9 8 7 6 5 4 3 2 1
Printed in the United States of America

This book is dedicated lovingly to my Lord, Jesus Christ, who is everything to me, to my mother, Ann, and my best friend, Ann, who stood with me through so much.

Contents

Preface ix

Foreword xi

Introduction xiii

1 The Sacrifice of Praise 1
   Sacrifice?, *2*
   The Sacrifice of Obedience, *4*
   The Sacrifice of Following Jesus, *5*
   A Living Sacrifice, *8*
   The Sacrifice of Praise, *11*

2 The Fellowship of
   the Holy Spirit 13
   Who Is the Holy Spirit?, *13*
   Why Do We Need the Holy Spirit?, *16*
   The Presence of the Holy Spirit, *19*
   The Benefits of His Presence, *24*

3 Communion With God 27
   How Do We Commune With God?, *27*
   Abraham Was a Friend of God, *29*
   The Fear of the Lord, *31*
   The Pursuit of Holiness, *36*

4 The Desires of the Heart 43
   Dreams and Destiny, *44*
   Death Comes Before Resurrection, *49*
   The Matter of the Heart, *53*
   Be Anxious for Nothing, *58*

5 GIVE AND IT SHALL BE GIVEN 63
    God Had Another Plan, *63*
    There Is Power in the Name of Jesus, *66*
    Abundant Life, *69*
    Let Go and Let God, *74*

CONCLUSION 79

PREFACE

As a child I was raised in the Catholic Church and attended a Catholic grammar school for eight years. My parents divorced when I was six years old and I have also been divorced, twice myself. In the late 1970s, I received Jesus Christ as my Lord and Savior, but five years later through a series of events, I ran from God and His call on my life. For seventeen years I battled a series of addictions and came close to death twice. The faster I ran from God the more of a mess my life became.

One day as I was in the car on my way to a Codependents Anonymous meeting, the Lord spoke to me through a song on a secular radio station I had playing. The presence of the Lord filled that car and I began to weep as I drove down the road. I knew my time of running was over and that I had come to the end of myself spiritually and emotionally. I rededicated my life to the Lord that day and almost immediately, God delivered me from cigarettes, alcohol, and drugs. I gave up my illicit relationships and began to attend a Spirit-filled church. Over the next several years, the Lord miraculously set me free from the pain of my past and gave me a new hope and dream.

The Bible says in Genesis 50:20 that what the enemy meant for my harm, God will use it for good. This is my prayer: that the testimony of God's grace in my life will be an encouragement to you and a reminder that He will be just as faithful in your life as He was in mine. May God bless you as you seek to know Him more and discover His will for your life.

Foreword

It is my honor to be Raeann Fitz's pastor. What a great woman! I believe you will enjoy this book—a testimony of God's miraculous power of transformation. In this, her first book, you will be touched by the unique honesty and refreshing style of a Christian who shoots straight and is not smothered in sophisticated "Christian-eze." Sit down, open up your heart, and be led through a journey that will inspire, instruct, and impart God's grace. Know that the words you read are the fruit of a life lived. My wife, Jeannie, and I believe in Raeann, we believe in this book, and we believe in your desire to grow and learn more of our Christ.

—Phil Munsey
Senior Pastor
Life Church
Mission Viejo, CA

INTRODUCTION

There is a greater hunger in today's world to know the nature of God than there has ever been in the history of the church. People are no longer satisfied with simply existing; they are desperate for peace in place of the constant turmoil plaguing them.

Sadly, due to the lack of mentors in the church today, a large number of people are floundering their way through their Christian walk. Christians today are desperate for someone to truly disciple them and to teach them how to live the abundant life filled with all the blessings God has set aside for them, that Jesus died so they could have. The Bible is overflowing with God's promises that largely go unclaimed because Christians lack the knowledge of how to obtain them.

Simply going to church twice a week was never enough for me; this never fully quenched my spiritual thirst. I turned to books and tapes to help me learn and fill that longing in my soul. I have hundreds of books and tapes on many different subjects. As my hunger to know God grew stronger, I turned to the Holy Spirit to be my mentor. When I submitted my heart to his direction, the Holy Spirit began to teach me and helped me to understand my God and Creator. I was so desperate to build a relationship with God, but my rational mind was greatly challenged by the fact that I couldn't physically see or touch God. With my personality type, I wanted to have all of my questions about God answered yesterday! Years later I still know so little about my Savior! We are still building that relationship day by day, minute by minute. The journey is incredible and filled with indescribable joy. I still find myself in awe each time I discover something new about the character and nature of God.

I am confident that the Lord did not bring me to this place, teach me all these things, and allow me to struggle during certain places in my life just for my own benefit. I feel strongly that He wants me to share how God has worked in my life so that other people can learn from my experiences. Living as a Christian in today's world is not easy but God has promised to give His people the strength to endure and conquer each challenge they may encounter. When God spoke to my heart about writing this book, I was shocked. I have never had the inclination to write a book in my life. I reminded the Lord that 99.9 percent of the books on my shelf have "Revs." in front of their names or initials behind them and I do not have either by my name. This did not seem to sway Him and the prompting I felt in my heart continued. I wrote this book based on *His* Word and *His* ability, not my own. The words in this book are *His* words to you, His church today.

If you are struggling to gain a deeper understanding of God, His character, nature and His will for your life, I pray that this book will prove to be an invaluable resource as you seek to grow in your faith. The Lord gave me the following commission;

to help prepare His people for the awesome plans He has ordained for them. He is waiting. Are you ready? Pray this prayer with me:

> *Lord, I want to know you more.*
>
> *Give me new revelations of who you are through the pages of this book. Give me ears to hear what your Holy Spirit is saying to me today.*
>
> *Draw me into a closer relationship with you, Father.*
>
> *I surrender my heart, my soul, my mind to you now.*
>
> *In Jesus' name, I pray. Amen.*

Chapter One

The Sacrifice of Praise

> *Through Him, therefore, let us constantly and at all times offer up to God a sacrifice of praise, which is the fruit of lips that thankfully acknowledge and confess and glorify His Name.*
>
> —Hebrews 13:15, AMP

Sacrifice. No one really likes that word. I find myself associating the word *sacrifice* with pain or the act of giving up something I care for a great deal. As a new Christian who had recently rededicated my life to Christ, I knew there would be many changes in my life and that it was not going to be church as usual anymore.

I also knew I was supposed to praise and worship the Lord. That was hard for me to do. I felt as if I could not break through to God on a spiritual level. I would sit in my "prayer chair", have my "prayer posture", and play my praise and worship CDs but simply going through the motions of how to worship the Lord was not the same as truly entering in to the presence of the Almighty God. I would put on my serious face, close my eyes, try to envision the Lord, and the next thing you know, I was asleep. Other times, the phone would ring, the cats would fight, or someone would stop by. Were my fledgling attempts to worship God frustrating? Yep. That must be why it is called a sacrifice.

Sacrifice?

A good overall definition of the word *sacrifice* is "to give something which costs you something; yourself, your time, your things, or your money." The Hebrew word, *zabach,* means "the offering of a life." God delights in things that cost us something. God wants us to give voluntarily, but He wants our gifts to be sacrifices given with reverent and obedient hearts. God certainly understands what it means to sacrifice; He sent his only son Jesus to die on a cross for the sins of the world.

When God asks us to sacrifice for him, it is not because he needs our money in tithes. God does not need anything.

> The earth is the LORD's and the fullness thereof, the world and those who dwell therein.
> —PSALM 24:1, RSV

Psalm 50:10 also says every animal in the forest is His and the cattle on a thousand hills. What God desires to see in our hearts is clearly described in Psalm 51:17 (NIV), which states:

> The sacrifices of God are a broken spirit; a broken and contrite heart.

Living as a Christian will not always be easy. God is not interested in our comfort. He is interested in building our character. Every day we are being conformed into the image of Jesus. In Galatians 5:22 Paul describes the fruit of the Holy Spirit, that is growing within us. These seeds of righteousness are planted in the hearts of believers when they are born again. They are love, joy, peace, patience, kindness, goodness, faithfulness, and self-control. The next time you are caught in traffic on the freeway, held up in the grocery line or at the post office instead of grumbling about how long it is taking, reflect for a moment on the character that God is developing in you and thank Him that He is teaching you to be more patient. God can use the most ordinary circumstances to bring us closer to Him and to teach us how to be more like Him. The process of sacrificing our own will for the will of God and submitting our hearts willingly to His authority is difficult but the reward is a deeper and more fruitful relationship with our God.

When trying to describe the role of trials and testing in our lives as Christians, I am often reminded of a story I once heard Joyce Meyer share about a man who saw a butterfly struggling to get out of its cocoon. He very carefully took a knife and slit open the cocoon and out came a beautiful butterfly. However, a couple minutes later, the butterfly died. God in His wisdom had perfectly designed the struggle the butterfly had to endure freeing itself from that cocoon to give the insect the right amount of stress on it's wings to strengthen them and prepare it to fly. As Christians we need the struggle to grow and to survive just as the butterfly does. The more we yield to the process and do not resist God's discipline, the more we grow. We may not like the day-to-day challenges but the results are well worth the sacrifice.

The Sacrifice of Obedience

The Bible tells us in Malachi 3:10 to bring all the tithes into the storehouse. A tithe is 10 percent of your income, which out of faithfulness and thankfulness to God, the Bible instructs Christians to give back to Him by means of giving to your home church or regular place of worship. The Lord gave me a revelation on the importance of tithing. He showed me that He was not trying to get something *from* me (after all He does not need anything), but that He was trying to get something to me. The Lord was concerned with whether or not I would be obedient to His Word and honor His command to tithe.

Hebrews 10:25 says not to forsake the assembling of yourselves together. There is a strength that comes to you when you fellowship with other believers. You need that to stay strong in your Christian walk. For some people, Sunday is their only day off and it can be very tempting to sleep. But if you go with an expectancy to hear a word from the Lord and seek His presence, then He will minister to you, refresh you, and strengthen you more than a couple extra hours of sleep could.

> This book of the law shall not depart out of your mouth, but you shall meditate on it day and night, that you may observe and do according to all that is written in it. For then you shall make your way prosperous, and then you shall deal wisely and have good success.
> —Joshua 1:8, AMP

The Lord wants us to read and study His Word. The Bible is God's love letter to His people. The Bible is a recipe for living the good life God wants us to have. A regular routine of Bible reading, study, worship, and fellowship is necessary for Christians who desire to grow in their faith and to develop a deeper more intimate relationship with Christ.

Above all things, the Lord delights in our obedience, no matter what area of our lives he may be focusing on at one particular time.

> Has the LORD as much delight in burnt offerings and sacrifices as in obeying the voice of the Lord? Behold, to obey is better than sacrifice...
> — SAMUEL 15:22, NASB

The Lord wants to bring you to a higher place. He's your Abba Father, and He knows what is best for you. Just as a father who wants his son to obey him when he tells him not to run into the street, the Lord desires to lead us in ways that are safe, fruitful and through paths of righteousness and blessing. God desires that His people live the life He has created for them to the fullest. Surrender your heart to His wisdom and will today. No, we may not understand why God is leading us through certain difficult paths at the time of our trial, but someday whether it be a week from now or twenty years later, God will reveal to us the purposes of our hardships and the rewards of our perseverance.

The Sacrifice of Following Jesus

To be a follower of Jesus requires more than a sacrifice of our will; at any given time you may be asked to let go of friendships, family relationships, or jobs. At times your relationship with Christ could cost you popularity, certain habits, or leisure activities that do not glorify God. Jesus said He did not come to bring peace, but a sword. (See Matthew 10:34–37.) Just as Jesus did not promise a life without trials, He also warned His followers that they would find opposition from unbelievers. He said a man's foes will be those of his own household. So why would you want to sacrifice so much to follow Jesus? It is because the value of giving it all up for Jesus will last an eternity, and the rewards both now and forever are endless.

In Luke 18:18–23 a rich young ruler asked Jesus how he could inherit eternal life. He said he obeyed all the commandments and did all the "right" things. Jesus told him to do one more thing; to sell all he had, give it to the poor, and come follow Him. Knowing he couldn't do that, the young ruler walked away discouraged because he had great wealth. Our Lord wants us to prosper, not to be poor. This example was purely to show the man where his heart was; his wealth came before his devotion to Jesus. The Lord knew his heart and the prominent place money held in his life. As Christian's we need to remember how easy it is to loose focus and to allow things other than God to dominate our affection. Our God is a jealous God, and he does not tolerate anything coming before Him in our lives.

I lived in a beautiful third floor condo in Florida for seventeen years. It had a gorgeous view of the river and mangroves, and the sun and the moon both rose over the water. There came a time in my life when I realized just how much that condo meant to me and I knew God was dealing with me about it.

One day, I got before the Lord and thanked Him for that beautiful place to live. Then I repented because I had placed the condo before Him in my heart, forgetting what a miracle it was to even purchase that condo in the first place. I wept until I came to the point where I was finally able to surrender the condo to the Lord. I was at a place that I was able to sincerely tell the Lord that I would sell my condo if that was His will for me and move wherever the Holy Spirit directed me. After I prayed that prayer, I wept even more. I think I know how Jacob felt when he wrestled with God in Genesis 32. I felt beat up and drained emotionally at the time. After that day, I began to feel differently about that condo. The condo no longer had the hold on me that it once did. It was hard to see at the time, but I definitely noticed it afterward. I actually felt like a tangible burden was lifted from my spirit. My priorities were now in order and I lived in that condo for several more years. I had peace in the end because God was again in His rightful place in my life—at the center of it.

I was the first one in my family to come to know Christ as Savior and I was single at the time. When that happened, some of my family members thought I had gotten involved in some type of a cult. There were times when I had to separate myself from my family. I had to tell them that Jesus came first in my life. One by one my family is coming into the kingdom, but first I had to get my priorities in order. God had to be my number one priority, and nothing or no one was going to come between us ever again.

As my priorities shifted into focus, I found my friends began to change as well. Old friends did not seem to call anymore, but God was faithful to bring in new friends who were believers in Christ as well to replace them. Because I was faithfully seeking Him, God blessed me with friends whose lives and relationships reflected the love of Jesus and a commitment to live by His Word. As I further surrendered my heart and desires to Him, He was faithful to meet all my needs spiritually, emotionally, and physically.

A Living Sacrifice

> I appeal to you therefore, brethren, and beg of you in view of [all] the mercies of God, to make a decisive dedication of your bodies [presenting all your members and faculties] as a living sacrifice, holy (devoted, consecrated) and well pleasing to God, which is your reasonable (rational, intelligent) service and spiritual worship.
>
> —ROMANS 12:1

To be a living sacrifice is to exhibit the character of Jesus Christ in everything we do and everywhere we go even when we are alone and no one else can see what we are doing. God is interested in our integrity; He sees what no one else can. I heard a speaker once say that she had just finished loading her groceries into the trunk of her car and the Holy Spirit told her to take the grocery cart back into the store instead of leaving it between cars.

The Holy Spirit began to deal with me about the same issue. I kept hearing her words over and over in my head, "take it back, take it back." When there was no designated grocery cart return area in the parking lot, I would walk that cart back into the store. There were times when I saw that there was no cart return area and I struggled with thirty-two plastic bags of groceries draped over both of my arms, breaking eggs and smashing bread just so I would not have to walk back to the store with that cart! No wonder God calls us a "peculiar people." (See 1 Peter 2:9.) We are quite lazy too!

The biggest testimony a person can have for Jesus Christ is in the daily life they lead. People watch you to see if your faith really matches up with your actions and lifestyle. Being a Christian in a world dominated by nonbelievers is similar to being examined and evaluated under a microscope. When I first came to the Lord, I had a lot of anger in my heart. God would use people like sandpaper to soften my rough edges as He worked within my heart to free me from the anger I had held onto for so much of my life.

> Iron sharpens iron, so one man sharpens another.
> —Proverbs 27:17, NASB

As He dealt with me regarding my anger, situations would develop that normally would send me over the edge. But as I felt my anger begin to rise, the Holy Spirit prompted me and reminded me of God's strength available to me to overcome the temptation to let my anger get out of control. One day, I looked back and realized the changes that had taken place in my heart. From that time forward, I did not battle anger the way I had before. God had set me free from that stronghold in my life. I had come to the point where I realized that my life would never be an effective witness to others about Christ if I could not control my anger and emotions.

Just as God wants us to lay our burdens down before Him, he also wants us to lay aside our personal goals, and aspirations. He wants us to put our energy and resources at His disposal, trusting Him to guide us and use those resources for His glory. Jeremiah 29:11 says that God has a wonderful plan for your life, to give you hope and a future (author's paraphrase).

God is the one who designed you and blessed you with talents and abilities in the first place. He just wants to use the talents He has given you for His glory. You have talents and abilities that you are not even aware of yet. If you offer yourself up to the Lord, He will develop them and put them to use.

When the Lord spoke to me about writing this book, I told Him He must have me mixed up with someone else (just kidding!). Honestly, though, that is just about how I felt because I was sure I did not have the ability to write a book. I looked at all the books on my bookshelf written by pastors, evangelists, and theologians many of whom have worldwide ministries. I had no initials behind my name or in front, but it was the Lord's ability working in and through me that enabled me to write this book. The only thing that God asks of us is that we are yielded vessels, ready to do His will. We must be willing to step out of the boat like Peter did in Matthew 14:22–35. I am willing to be that living sacrifice that is able to deliver the message He wants to bring to His people of this generation. What about you? Are you willing to let Him stir up the gifts and talents He has placed deep within you? Are you willing to have your life be a living epistle read of all men? (See 2 Corinthians 3:2.) You can trust God to be faithful! Step out in faith and lay your life down as a sacrifice to God! You will not regret it!

The Sacrifice of Praise

The enemy will throw distractions at you to keep you from worshiping and praising God. He does not want you to draw closer to the Lord because he knows what tremendous power becomes available to you through a life surrendered to God. With obedience, great power is released: the power to overcome, prosper, serve God, and resist temptation.

Once you begin to let God be God and have His way in your life, your heart will overflow with thankfulness for all the wonderful things God is doing in you and through you. The greatest reason we should praise and thank Him is for the glorious sacrifice that Jesus made for us in giving His innocent life in exchange for taking on the sins of the world. How wonderful it is to tell others what the Lord has done in our lives! When we show acts of kindness to others, are obedient to God's commands, and live with integrity, we are offering up a sacrifice of praise to God.

Chapter Two

THE FELLOWSHIP OF THE HOLY SPIRIT

Who Is the Holy Spirit?

Everyone enjoys times of fellowship with somebody whether it is a husband and wife, children, parents, friends, relatives, coworkers, etc. Spending quality time together is one way humans show affection for each other and how we grow into deeper relationships with those around us.

In this chapter, I want to help you understand how you can enter into fellowship with the Holy Spirit. First, we have to know a little bit about Him. The Holy Spirit *is* God. He is the third person in the Trinity. He is as much "God" as God the Father and God the Son (Jesus). He is equal in majesty, power, and glory.

> Now the Lord is the Spirit, and where the Spirit of the Lord is, there is liberty (emancipation from bondage, freedom).
>
> —2 Corinthians 3:17

He is the voice of God to you. He hears the Father and speaks directly to you. (See John 16:13.)

Jesus was speaking with His disciples in John chapter 14 to comfort them and let them know that it was good for Him to leave this earth so that the Father could send the Holy Spirit who would abide with them and teach them all things. That is where the Holy Spirit abides, here with us on earth, in our hearts. The Father and the Son (Jesus) are in heaven, but the Holy Spirit walks the earth.

When a baby is born, not only do the parents pick a name that they like for that child, but often times they find out what that name means. For example, the name *Ann* means "gracious," and the name *John* means "God is gracious." In the Old Testament, God often changed the names of people like Abram. *Abram* meant "high, exalted father," but God changed it to *Abraham,* which meant "the father of a multitude." In Genesis 12:2, God promised to make Abram a great nation and to bless him and make him a blessing. In Genesis 17, God affirmed that word by changing his name to Abraham and giving Abraham the vision of what he was to become—the father of a multitude. In essence, God gave him a new assignment and a new name.

A name usually speaks of characteristics or traits you would want a person to have, which sometimes can end up being a self-fulfilling prophecy. My best friend's name is Ann and she is the most gracious person I have ever known. She has truly taken on the characteristic her name embodies.

In this part of the chapter let us explore the names of the Holy Spirit as they are given in the

Bible. This will tell us a little bit about who the Holy Spirit is. The Holy Spirit is a real person with feelings and emotions. He hates to be grieved, insulted, blasphemed, resisted, lied to, or quenched. God sent His Spirit to earth to help, to teach, to guide, to fill, and to anoint us.

The first place He appears in the Bible is in Genesis 1:2 where the Spirit of God hovered over the face of the waters. In Isaiah 59:19, He is the Spirit of the Lord. When God the Father refers to the Holy Spirit, He is "My Spirit" as found in Joel 2:28. In Luke 1:35 He is the Power of the Most High, the Spirit of Christ in I Peter 1:11 and in Philippians 1:19 as well as Galatians 4:6-7.

Now let us take a look at what the Bible says are some of His attributes:

- The Spirit of grace and supplication—Zechariah 12:10.
- The Spirit of wisdom and understanding—Isaiah 11:2.
- The Spirit of counsel and might—Isaiah 11:2.
- The Spirit of knowledge and of the fear of the Lord—Isaiah 11:2.
- The Spirit of adoption—Romans 8:14-15.
- The Spirit of life—Romans 8:2.
- The Spirit of grace—Hebrews 10:29.
- The Holy Spirit of promise—Ephesians 1:13.
- The Spirit of truth—John 14:17.

- The Spirit of holiness—Romans 1:4.
- The Spirit of prophecy—Revelation 19:10.
- The eternal Spirit—Hebrews 9:14.
- The Spirit of glory—1 Peter 4:14.
- The Comforter—John 14:16.

The Amplified Bible further expands the term *comforter* with "counselor, advocate, helper, intercessor, strengthener, and standby." He is absolutely everything we need.

In Acts 2:2 the Holy Spirit is depicted as a mighty rushing wind and in the next verse as cloven tongues resembling fire. In Ezekiel 47:1–12, the Holy Spirit is metaphorically described as water. When Jesus was baptized by John in Matthew 3:16, the Holy Spirit descended on Him from heaven as a dove.

There is much that can be written about the Holy Spirit. If you are interested into delving deeper, I would suggest reading the books *Good Morning Holy Spirit* and *Welcome Holy Spirit* both by Benny Hinn. These are excellent books and provide great revelation and insight into the person of the Holy Spirit.

Why Do We Need the Holy Spirit?

Romans chapter 8 sums up many of the reasons why we need the Holy Spirit.

- He will give you power over sin (vv. 1–2).
- He will fulfill the laws of Moses (the Ten Commandments), which will give us freedom (vv. 3–4).
- He will give us the mind of God giving us

life, peace and the ability to please God (vv. 5–8).
- He gives us righteousness or right standing with God (vv. 9–10).
- He gives life and health to our mortal body (v. 11).
- He brings death to self and our sinful nature (vv. 12–14).
- He will help us testify of our salvation (vv. 15–16).

Without the help of the Holy Spirit, it is impossible to live a successful Christian life. Satan is a very real foe who hates God's people and does everything he possibly can to lure them back into a sinful life. When I wasn't walking in the power of the Holy Spirit, wasn't reading my bible, wasn't praying and fellowshiping with Him, I left a door open for the devil. Satan fooled me, lied to me, and drew me away from the Lord for seventeen years. I became involved in every destructive behavior possible. Even though I was away from God, He never left me. Looking back, I can see how His mighty hand protected me, twice from death, and mostly from myself. For years, I had dreams that I was running so fast that I would become airborne and fly. I am confident these dreams were from the Holy Spirit who was trying to get my attention. But I wasn't listening.

Then one day in my car on my way to a Codependents Anonymous meeting, the Holy Spirit spoke to me through a song by Amy Grant, a Christian recording artist that was playing on my *secular* radio station. The whole song was like a loud speaker going off in my head. Somehow I knew that God was speaking to me. I began to sob as the presence of the Lord filled my car. I turned around and went back home, repented before God, and recommitted my life to Him. I will never forget that day.

From that day forward, the Holy Spirit began to change me from the inside out. He comforted me and gave me hope; I felt alive again instead of dead on the inside and I knew that with God in control everything was going to be okay. As my depression lifted, I began to feel peace. My entire outlook on life changed. I felt stronger on the inside and a freedom I had never experienced before. As the Holy Spirit worked in my heart, I did not want to swear, or drink, or smoke any longer. I was so grateful to God for a second chance. I knew that God was at work and my spirit was being transformed and renewed everyday. I found myself wanting to tell everyone what was going on inside of me. The Holy Spirit began to lead me, guide me, and teach me in the ways of the Father. He would speak to me while I was working or reading the Word or while I was listening to a sermon. The Holy Spirit was directing me on how to overcome my fears and deal with my issues. He even brought healing to me twice through episodes of "Touched by an Angel" on television. I always used to have noise in the house to drown out my thoughts, either the stereo or TV. I turned them off so I could hear the voice of the Holy Spirit talking to me and I began to live expectantly for the next word or revelation.

Without the Holy Spirit, communion between God

and man is not possible. You do not have to go through seventeen years in the wilderness in order to meet Him. All you have to do is ask. He stands at *your* door and knocks. (See Revelation 3:20.) Invite the Holy Spirit in; surrender! Do not live a minute longer without the fullness of the Holy Spirit in your life.

The Presence of the Holy Spirit

When I was first accepted Christ as my Savior, I would hear people talk about the "presence of God." I used to wonder what they were talking about. I am the type of person who does not notice things about myself most of the time. For instance, I do not like going to the doctor, so if I was still sick after three weeks, I would break down and make an appointment. Most of the time when I did go to the doctor, he would ask me about other related symptoms I might have and most of my answers were that I had not noticed. When people would talk to me about how strong the presence of God was in a service, I usually did not feel or notice anything.

One day an evangelist came to my church. After the service, he called those forward who needed prayer. I went up because I had a bad headache. As he began to pray for people and lay his hands on them, they began to fall to the ground. I was raised in the Catholic Church and I was not familiar with this particular experience sometimes referred to as being "slain in the Spirit." Since bolting to the door was too obvious and since I was too scared to move anyhow, I decided to endure this man knowing that *I* surely was not going to fall.

My turn came to be prayed for and the next thing

I know, somebody is picking me up off the floor. I did not feel or notice anything. I heard everything that was going on around me, but I couldn't move or open my eyes. I am good at rationalizing, so I thought for sure that this was not God but fear. Nothing really changed at the time until I noticed something about a week later. Throughout most of my teenage years and up until that day, I suffered from migraine headaches. They had escalated to the point where I was having an average of five or six each week. Since my experience of being "slain in the Spirit," I had not had a single migraine headache and to this day, I hardly ever get one.

While I was not sure what I had experienced at the time, I later came to understand that what I had referred to as "falling" was simply spending time anointed with the power and presence of the Holy Spirit. Again, this is what is often referred to as "being slain in the Spirit" or "falling under the power." In Daniel 10:8–9, Daniel "retained no strength" and "fell into a deep sleep on his face, with his face to the ground." In Revelation 1:17, John saw a vision that made him "fall at His [Jesus'] feet as if dead." On the Damascus road, Paul (Saul at the time) fell to the ground as a heavenly light shone around him. (See Acts 9:4.) I do not believe I had to fall to be healed of those migraines. However, God chose to heal me that way. He is sovereign and can do whatever He chooses, and we do not have to understand why. He definitely got my attention that day.

There are many things that happen to people under the power of God. Some people have seen visions of the Lord, others have had ministry calls and still others have been healed from physical ailments, delivered from drugs or alcohol, and some receive the baptism of the Holy Spirit (more on this later). The presence of God is so powerful that our mortal bodies can only take so much. That is why one feels so weak when they arise or are "drunk in the Spirit" as many call it.

Some of the other manifestations of the presence of Holy Spirit are:

- Tingling sensations almost as if you were shivering
- Heat either all over your body or a certain area of your body
- The feeling of hot oil being poured over your head and down your body
- Weightiness or like a heavy blanket was thrown over you
- Numbness
- Uncontrollable shaking
- Dizziness or lightheadedness
- Extreme peace
- Weeping

Man was separated from God back in the Garden of Eden because of sin. The shed blood of Jesus has once again reconciled us to God. That is why we must repent of our sins and be born again. (See John 3:16.)

> Through Him [Jesus] we both have our access in one Spirit to the Father.
> —EPHESIANS 2:18, NASB

The Holy Spirit brings us into the presence of God. One time in the presence of God and you will never be the same again.

Benny Hinn is a powerful man of God with an international saving and healing ministry. The first time I saw him on TV, I was not sure about him because I did not know anything about his ministry. I happened to be watching his program one day and when he shouted the word "fire," the power of God shot through that TV set and pinned me against the back of the couch. Forty-five minutes later when I could move again, all I could think was "wow, it is real."

I knew that the power of God was present in those crusades. Needless to say, the next time he came within driving distance, I went to his crusade. One of the many things I remember about that crusade is that I did not bring enough Kleenex; all I did was cry and shake during the entire meeting. I had never experienced the presence of the Lord like that in my life. That night I could not sleep because there was tingling racing up and down my entire body. This went on for a week. Five other people from my church attended the crusade and none of them had this same experience.

My life was never the same after that meeting. My hunger and desire for more of God intensified. I read my Bible like never before, watched powerful men of God on TV, prayed and worshiped every chance I had, and devoured books and tapes about the Lord. My whole life was turned around, not by a man, but by the power of the Holy Spirit and the presence of the Most High God. My prayer life was different, I was so in love with God, I was thankful for everything, I loved differently, I felt a surge of power like they felt in Acts 1:8. God began to use me and give me direction. He equipped me to serve and gave me a ministry. I found there was a heavenly song running through my head all the time, and the word of the Lord began to flow from my mouth every time I spoke.

You do not have to attend a crusade like the one I did to get into the presence of God. You can feel it in your own home as you pray and listen to worship music. Just as God is everywhere, His Spirit dwells within our hearts and we are able to commune with Him anywhere, anytime.

> Every Scripture is God-breathed (given by His inspiration) and profitable for instruction, for reproof and conviction of sin, for correction of error and discipline in obedience, [and] for training in righteousness (in holy living, in conformity to God's will in thought, purpose, and action).
>
> —2 Timothy 3:16

God says He is the "I AM," not the "I was" or "I will be."

Since sin originally separated us from the presence of God, sin can also keep us from the presence of God even after salvation. The Bible clearly lists the things God sees as sin. Galatians 5:19–21, 1 Corinthians 6:9–10, Ephesians 5:5, and 1 Peter 3:12 are just a few scripture references to give you an idea of what God hates. We must be quick to repent of any sin in our lives on a daily basis. I repent immediately when I know I have sinned. I don't want to take a chance of forgetting. I have even locked myself in a public restroom to get right with God. The presence of God brings His gentle conviction of sin. In the Book of Acts, His presence also brings His power.

The Benefits of His Presence

The Book of Acts is a record of the changes that happened in the lives of the apostles because of their fellowship with the Holy Spirit. When you welcome the Holy Spirit into your life and yield to Him, these same changes will occur in your life. Acts 10:34 says that God is no respecter of persons. He loves us all equally and each one of us is just as capable of being used by God in the same ways the apostles were used by God. Let us go over some of the changes that you can expect in your life as you spend time in the presence of God and in fellowship with the Holy Spirit based on what we see in the Book of Acts. I would encourage you to read the Book of Acts if you have not read it lately.

As you draw closer to the Lord and spend time in His presence, you will begin to hear differently. Not only will you hear with your ears, you will begin to hear with your heart or have spiritual hearing. Your heart will become especially sensitive to the prompting of the Holy Spirit. Your speech will change as well. When the Holy Spirit came upon the apostles in Acts 2:4, "They began to speak with other tongues, [languages] as the Spirit was giving them utterance" (NAS). This verse causes a lot of confusion and dissension between people of different denominational backgrounds.

Some denominations believe the "baptism of the Holy Spirit" or speaking in tongues ended when the apostles died. Back when the Lord touched me and I was healed from migraine headaches, I also began to notice strange words rambling around in my head. I thought that I was mimicking the words I heard my pastor speak when he prayed in his "heavenly language." I knew that they definitely were not something I had learned in French class in high school. I began to speak them out when I was alone in my car. As more words came, I began to have a desire to utter these words.

Tongues is an unknown heavenly language given to you by the Holy Spirit as a manifestation or evidence that you have been baptized in the Holy Spirit. First Corinthians 14:2 says, "For one who speaks in an [unknown] tongue speaks not to men but to God, for no one understands or catches his meaning, because in the [Holy] Spirit he utters secret truths and hidden things [not obvious to the understanding]." The baptism of the Holy Spirit brings power into your life. Your mind feels renewed, your spirit free, your body refreshed, and your witness for Christ becomes bold and powerful. You are drawn to pray in that heavenly language and in your own language as the Spirit leads you.

Because of the power and freedom you now experience, your whole appearance begins to change. Your eyes sparkle and you feel strong physically. In Acts 4:13, the people saw the "boldness of Peter and John" (NKJV). You will develop the boldness to come before God in your prayers and petitions, boldness with people and in your witness, and boldness against

Satan. You will experience things you never thought possible. New authority will come into your life.

The Holy Spirit will change your vision; what you see and how you see; your sense of discernment will increase and you will desire the leading of the Holy Spirit as you welcome Him as a partner in decision-making and trust your own judgment less often. Attitudes will change. Your outlook, prayer life, and your direction will change as well as your understanding and insight which will increase. Influence and leadership abilities will increase. Basically, you are in for a glorious overhaul. I welcomed the presence of the Holy Spirit into my life because I did not like who I was on the inside. My bad habits and attitudes did not change overnight, but they did change. God deals with each of us on His schedule and in His time. We will never fully "arrive" spiritually before we leave this earth. Paul says in 2 Corinthians 3:18 (NASB) that we are "being transformed into the same image from glory to glory, just as from the Lord, the Spirit." This all comes by fellowshiping with the Holy Spirit and spending time in His presence.

When Moses came down from Mount Sinai after being in the presence of the Lord, his face shone so brightly that he had to put a veil over his face to talk with the children of Israel. (See Exodus 34:29–35). The presence of the Lord within you will ooze into every area of your life becoming evident in all your actions and how you live your life. Ask the Lord for the baptism of the Holy Spirit, spend time reading the Word of God, and seek His presence. It will change your life.

Chapter Three

Communion With God

Communion with God is much more than partaking in the Lord's Supper with bread and wine. It is personal, intimate, friendship with God. Communion with God is learning to understand the very heart of God.

How Do We Commune With God?

Your physical body is the part of you that is in contact with the earthly things of this world. Your soul is the part of you that feels, understands, thinks, and decides; but it is your spirit that communes with God. In the last chapter, we discussed two of the meanings of communion - presence and fellowship. Some of the other meanings of communion are:

- **Friendship**: The Spirit of God longs to be your closest friend; someone whom you can trust with your deepest secrets and with your heart.

- **Intimacy**: Webster describes this as "marked by a very close association, contact, or familiarity; a warm friendship developed through a long association."[1]
- **Sharing together**: You tell Him what is on your heart, He tells you what is on His heart.
- **Working together**: The Holy Spirit becomes your partner in everything you do.
- **Companionship**: The Holy Spirit is someone you trust and respect to speak into your life and guide you because He knows what is best for you.

Communion involves two-way conversations. For many years I would come to the Lord with my "wish" lists, pray for Him to watch over my family and friends, thank Him, and say Amen. I never waited and listened long enough to hear what He had to say to me. If you had a friend that would only call you to talk about their problems or needs and never stopped to listen to what was going on in your life or show any concern for your well-being, you would not want to continue that relationship, would you? That friendship could never really grow into anything meaningful.

The Lord created us for friendship and communion with Him. Adam walked with the Lord in the cool of the day in the garden in Genesis 3:8 and Moses met with the Lord face to face in Exodus 33:11. Jesus even calls us friends in John 15:15.

Learning to hear the voice of the Lord takes practice. Elijah describes the voice of the Lord as a "still, small voice" (1 Kings 19:12, NKJV). He speaks to your very conscience or your "inner man." Romans 9:1 says, "my conscience [enlightened and prompted] by the Holy Spirit bearing witness with me." You will know that voice on the inside. It is not booming, but gentle, and usually brings peace and an assurance that you have just heard from God. I keep my spiritual ears open all the time, fearful that I will miss a word, direction, or a warning from the Lord. As Christians, it is imperative that our spirits be tuned to the voice of the Lord at all times.

Abraham Was a Friend of God

Let's take a look at one of God's friends in the Bible and how he communed with God. Abraham is one of my favorite Bible figures. We first meet Abraham (Abram before God changed his name) in Genesis 12. He was a very wealthy livestock owner who lived somewhere around 2091 B.C. Abraham was seventy-five years old when God asked him to leave his country, his relatives, and his father's house and go to a place the Lord would show him. He had no children, but he took his wife Sarah (Sarai before God changed her name), his nephew Lot, his possessions, and servants and went to live in the land of Canaan. He had to choose between the security of what he already had and the uncertainty of traveling under God's direction.

Abraham was obedient in everything God had asked him to do; therefore, God made him a promise. God promised Abraham that He would bless him and make him a mighty nation, that He would bless all his *descendants* with land, possessions, and prosperity.

How could this be? He was seventy-five years old and had no children. Romans 4:3 says, "Abraham believed in God, and it was credited to his account as righteousness."

Abraham was a great man of faith and he believed that what God said would come to pass even when the circumstances looked impossible. This type of faith can only come by communing with God and knowing His nature and character. He was a man of great prayer who would regularly worship God. He took the time to get to know God. James 2:23 further adds that Abraham "was called God's friend" (NIV).

At the age of one hundred years old (his wife, Sarah, was ninety), the promise of God came to pass in Abraham's life, and Isaac was born. Through his lineage, all the nations of the world were blessed, and he became the founder of the Jewish nation.

This wasn't the end of Abraham's testing by God. When Isaac was about 13, God told Abraham to sacrifice Isaac as a burnt offering. (See Genesis 22.) The next morning, Abraham set out on a three-day journey with Isaac to the place God had told him. There he built an altar, tied up his son, and was ready to slay him when the angel of the Lord called to him from heaven and told him to put his knife down. The angel of the Lord went on to say that He knew Abraham feared (reverenced) God enough not to withhold his only son from Him. Since Abraham believed the promises God had made him, he also knew that God was able to raise Isaac up from the dead to fulfill those promises. (See Hebrews 11:19.)

What great faith, but what great tests! The Bible says that to whom much is given, much is required.

(See Luke 12:48.) To receive all the blessings that God has for you will require faith and an intimate friendship with God. But how do we get there? Psalm 25:14 says, "Friendship with the Lord is reserved for those who *fear* Him. With them He shares the secrets of His covenant." Are we to fear Him?

The Fear of the Lord

When you hear the word *fear*, you relate it to being afraid. The Hebrew word *yare* means "to fear or to *reverence*." God does not want us to be afraid of Him. Proverbs 8:13 says, "The reverent fear and worshipful awe of the Lord [includes] the hatred of evil; pride, arrogance, the evil way, and perverted and twisted speech." In other words, it includes having God's attitude toward sin, not only in the lives of others, but especially in your own life.

I remember one time that I was tempted to lie for the sake of my friend in order to save her some money. The Spirit of the Lord was restraining me, but I outright lied anyway. I was a young Christian and had recently led this friend to the Lord. All of a sudden, this wave of guilt washed over me. I ran to the bathroom and began to cry. I asked the Lord to forgive me, I forgave myself, and asked my friend to forgive me. She knew how terrible I felt. This may not sound all that significant to you, but to me it was traumatic. It wasn't only the fact that I lied, but that I had hurt God. When you begin to understand the holiness of God, the last thing you want to do is to knowingly disappoint Him. This is what is meant by "reverential fear," and it was a turning point in my life because *now* I truly *feared* the Lord.

Leviticus 19:2 (NASB) says, "You shall be holy, for I the Lord your God am holy." God has no tolerance toward sin and neither should we. No matter how unholy we are now, or how impossible it may seem for us to become holy, if we have committed our lives to the Lord Jesus Christ and He is living within us, we need to remember *He* is holy. If we choose to walk in obedience to the next thing He tells us to do, His holy life will start to be manifest through us.

> Let all the earth fear the Lord [revere and worship Him]; let all the inhabitants of the world stand in awe of Him. For He spoke, and it was done, He commanded, and it stood fast.
> —PSALM 33:8–9, NASB

He created this universe and everything in it. How can you not be in awe of how great our God really is? He measures the waters of the world in the palm of His hand. (See Isaiah 40:12.) Now that is awesome.

We have already reviewed the names of the Holy Spirit in chapter 2; now let's go over some of the Hebrew names of God and their meanings in order to understand how truly awesome He is.

- Yahweh is God's proper name and hard to describe. Some believe the meaning to be "I AM" (Exodus 3:14) or "the Lord" (Exodus 20:7).

- El-Shaddai—God Almighty (Genesis 17:1)

- El-Elyon—God, the Most High God (Genesis 14:18)

- Adonai—my Lord and my Master (Genesis 15:2)

- Elohim—your God (Isaiah 41:10)
- Jehovah-Jireh—my Provider (Genesis 22:14)
- Jehovah-Rophe—my Healer (Exodus 15:26)
- Jehovah-M'Kaddesh—the Lord my Sanctifier (Leviticus 20:8)
- Jehovah-Nissi—my Banner of Salvation (Exodus 17:15)
- Jehovah-Shalom—my Peace (Judges 6:24)
- Jehovah-Tsidkenu—my Righteousness (Jeremiah 23:6)
- Jehovah-Rohi—my Shepherd (Psalm 23:1)
- El 'Olam—the Eternal or Everlasting One (Psalm 90:2)
- Yahweh Tseba'oth—the Lord of hosts (1 Samuel 1:3)
- Jehovah-Ro'i—the One who sees (Genesis 16:3)
- El Gibbor—Mighty God (Isaiah 9:6)
- Yahweh Shammah—the Lord is there (Ezekiel 48:35)

This is only a partial list. He is the God of *everything* you need. Are you in awe yet? Hopefully I have created for you a picture of a God that you can no longer take lightly. We as humans will never truly be able to comprehend the magnitude and greatness of God.

The fear of the Lord should do two things for us.

First, give us the same attitude toward sin that God has, and second, create a deep respect in us for the holiness of God, the power of God, and His ability to completely meet our needs.

To fear God is to believe Him. To believe God is to obey Him. The fear of the Lord is directly connected to obedience. Sometimes God will ask us to do things that do not make any sense at all. We do not need to understand why, we just need to understand the nature of God and that we can trust Him. This was the case with Abraham when God asked him to offer up his son Isaac as a burnt offering. God was testing Abraham to see how obedient he would be even when faced with sacrificing his own beloved son. He passed. He did not live long enough to see all the rewards that were promised to him and his descendants. But to this day, the promises that God made to Abraham can still be seen because of his obedience to several seemingly illogical requests. Abraham is even listed in the genealogy of Jesus.

The fear of the Lord is the only way to be released from the fear of man. The fear of man is being more concerned with what man thinks of your actions than you are of what God thinks of them. This is bondage, plain and simple.

> The fear of man brings a snare, but whoever leans on, trusts in, and puts his confidence in the Lord is safe and is set on high.
> —PROVERBS 29:25, AMP

All my life (especially during my seventeen years in the "wilderness") I had a fear of man and felt that I needed to be all things to all people. If they were sad, I had to cheer them up. If they invited me out, I had to go. If they needed money, I found some; whatever the need, I managed to fulfill it. The word *no* was not in my vocabulary. I was my biggest critic. I hated the roller coaster and I wanted to get off.

I was dating a man during those years for whom I could not do enough to earn his respect or his love. After two years of trying, I couldn't take it anymore and I broke up with him. I was devastated but I had to do it. I became very depressed and went on antidepressant medication. I then decided to see a therapist. She was wonderful in that she gave me a name for this torment I was in—codependency. That means that my fear had caused me to be controlled by him. My identity was swallowed up by his, and I was acting no different than if I was addicted to alcohol or drugs. Just knowing it had a name was a relief and that others suffered with this problem, too. I was not crazy after all! Codependency was an addiction I had used to fill the void in my life because I felt unworthy and unlovable. I began to attend meetings with other people experiencing the same problems. This was the same meeting I was going to on October 16th when the Lord spoke to me in my car through a song on the radio. I no longer needed twelve steps to get me through this thing, just one, and His name is Jesus. James 4:8 says, "come near to God and He will come near to you" (NIV). I ran to Him and immediately, I noticed a change. I felt so light. The total change didn't happen overnight, but it did happen. I was so glad to be free from that bondage.

Little by little, what God thought about me

became more important to me than what anyone thought about me. I did not become rude or insensitive, but I did gain a proper perspective. This was a freedom that I had never experienced before. I was truly in awe of God. From there I went on a quest to pursue Him and learn of His holiness.

The Pursuit of Holiness

Holy and *holiness* appear over 900 times in the Bible. The Bible describes in Revelation 4:8 and Isaiah 6:3 how the angels in heaven gather around the throne of God in worship. The angels fly around the throne day and night saying, "Holy, holy, holy is the Lord God Almighty, who was, and is, and is to come" (NIV). We will never understand God's mercy until we understand His holiness. Mercy means not getting what we deserve. We deserved death, but Jesus gave us life.

God will never do anything that is contrary to His nature. There is no sin in Him. He is perfect. God's holiness is our standard for holy living. God is a holy God and He wants His people to be holy and to walk blamelessly before Him.

> But as the One who called you is holy, you yourselves also be holy in all your conduct and manner of living.
> —1 PETER 1:15

Holiness means "to be consecrated from what is unclean and dedicated to what is clean and pure." Second Corinthians 7:1 (KJV) says, "Dearly beloved, let us cleanse ourselves from all filthiness of the flesh and spirit, perfecting holiness in the fear of God."

Because God is holy, He cannot excuse, ignore, or tolerate sin. Sin separates us from God. People who die with their sins unforgiven separate themselves from God eternally. God wants them to live with Him in heaven, but He cannot take them into His holy presence unless their sin has been removed. Jesus, taking our place on the cross, made a way for mortal, sinful man to approach the throne of God in heaven.

No matter how hard we try, our sinful nature will always be present. We need the help of the Holy Spirit to give us power over sin because we cannot strive towards holiness on our own.

> …by the sanctifying work of the Spirit, to obey Jesus Christ.
>
> —1 Peter 1:2, nasb

Sanctification is the process by which Christians grow in holiness and are cleansed, set apart, and made holy. We don't become sanctified overnight, but as Christians we are constantly growing closer to God and purifying our hearts.

> May the God of peace Himself sanctify you entirely.
>
> —1 Thessalonians 5:23, nasb

Back in the late 1970s and early 1980s, there was a nighttime soap opera on TV on Friday nights. I would arrange my whole week around that show. It had the usual story lines: adultery, infidelity, murder, revenge, stealing, lying, etc. I really got involved with the story wondering what would happen from week to week. I would literally be consumed by that show for an hour. Eventually, a change began to happen in my heart. The Lord began removing the desire to watch that program from me and He was ever so gentle about it. I missed one Friday night because of an engagement I couldn't get out of and realized that watching the show was not that important after all. From that point forward I made the decision not to watch it anymore. I even began to hate the appearance of evil that the show portrayed.

It is so important to be careful what you watch or what you hear. Those images stay in your mind and are played back over and over again and can lead us into temptation and sin. I heard one pastor call them our "eye gates" and our "ear gates." In order to walk in holiness, we must protect our ears, our eyes and our hearts from unholy images, words and subjects. Another pastor from Argentina once said that the Lord told him that 98 percent holiness wasn't good enough. He said it was like drinking a glass of water that contained 98 percent purified water and 2 percent sewer water in it. Would you drink that? I certainly would not want to!

Leukemia begins with a genetic change in a single white blood cell. From that one cell mutating a potentially deadly disease can take hold in a person's body with lethal consequences. Sin pollutes and permeates our lives in much the same way as the cancer. A little white lie here, a little lust there, you allow yourself to envy a friend or a colleague. Before you are aware of it, your heart has been overtaken by sinful thoughts and desires, which the Bible clearly says will lead to death if we do not surrender our lives to Christ and ask Him to forgive us of our sin.

As you grow in holiness, you will notice that when

you do sin, you want to make it right immediately. The Bible uses another word: repentance. Repentance is more than just confessing your sin to God and saying that you are sorry. To repent means "to turn away from or go another way." Repentance is a permanent change of heart, of mind, and of your life toward sin.

> Godly sorrow brings repentance that leads to salvation and leaves no regret, but worldly sorrow brings death.
> —2 CORINTHIANS 7:10, NIV

Repentance is saying to God that you are truly remorseful and will not do it again no matter what. We as humans are incapable of never sinning again, but it is the attitude of holiness and repentance and our willingness to turn away from sin that God is concerned with.

If there is sin in our life that we have overlooked, the Holy Spirit will gently *convict* us of it. (See John 16:8.) God speaks very specifically and directly, and His Word is very clear. If there is ever any feeling of *guilt*, it is not from God. Satan is called the "accuser of the brethren" in the Bible (Rev. 12:10) and will attack you with feelings of guilt and condemnation. When he tries to make you feel guilty about past sin, firmly stand on the Word of God and refuse to allow Satan's lies to affect you. As born again believers in Jesus Christ, we have authority over him. Satan is powerless to harm you, and he must submit to Christ's authority.

> Submit yourselves, then, to God. Resist the devil, and he will flee from you.
> —JAMES 4:7, NIV

Sin in our lives is reflective of what is going on in our minds and hearts. As Christians we need to adjust our thought patterns. Philippians 4:8 (NIV) reminds us of this:

> Finally, brothers, whatever is true, whatever is noble, whatever is right, whatever is pure, whatever is lovely, whatever is admirable—if anything is excellent or praiseworthy—think about such things.

Guard what you see, hear, and what you allow yourself to be exposed to.

Are you holding onto any unforgiveness towards anyone? Do you need to ask anyone for forgiveness? Are you in a relationship that violates the laws of God? Is there anything in your life that you have placed before God? Are there any addictions in your life? As believers in Christ desiring to grow in our knowledge and relationship with him, we must constantly be examining our hearts for unconfessed sin. As you submit to His work in your life, the Holy Spirit will gently show you areas that need to be addressed. Be patient with yourself. Let God help you with the changes. Get real with God. Bear your heart to Him. He knows everything about you anyway. This is how you develop a deep and intimate relationship with the Lord. You speak to Him and He speaks back to you. Draw close to Him and He will draw close to you. (See James 4:8.) Do not be afraid. If your heart is ready and willing, you will hear the voice of God.

As you grow in holiness, as you develop the fear of the Lord, as you read your Bible more and begin to know your Jesus better, you will find yourself eager to commune with God. You become eager to hear what the Lord has to say next or what He will show you next. Worshiping Him becomes a joy for you because you are so thankful for what God has done in your life that you want to praise Him for it. He becomes your "Abba" Father (Gal. 4:6) and you trust Him, and lean on Him for all your needs. He gives you things that you have not even asked for because He loves you so much and because He knows your needs ahead of time, before you even know them yourself. Do not be afraid, step out in faith and love God back with all your heart.

---

1 *Merriam Webster's Collegiate Dictionary*, 10th Edition (Springfield, MA: Merriam-Webster, Inc., 1998). It is the Holy Spirit that brings you into that deep place of intimacy with Christ. Romans 5:5 says, "God's love has been poured out into our hearts through the Holy Spirit who has been given to us."

Chapter Four

The Desires of the Heart

To desire is "to long for, want, or hope for." Older English versions of the Bible use synonyms such as "ask" and "seek." Desires are a basic part of life. The important issue is how you respond to your desires. Desires can control one's conduct, or they can be used to fulfill God's appointed purposes. The difference between a good and a bad desire is whether it is self-centered or a desire for God's will. The Bible tells us that the essence of sin is defined as "a determination to have one's own way." Evil desire is not necessarily a desire for something that is wicked, but it is a desire to have one's own way and putting one's self in the place of God. However, when God is someone's greatest desire, all that person's other desires become prioritized and then mirror God's desires for that person's own well-being. That is what Psalm 37:4 says:

Delight yourself also in the Lord, and He will give you the desires and secret petitions of your heart.

That is a promise.

We all know the story of David and Goliath. David was a giant killer and a king of Israel. Since he was a man after God's own heart (Acts 13:22), most of his desires lined up with God's desires. On the other hand, King Saul was very self-willed and stubborn and was removed from his throne as king of Israel by God because of his wicked ways and sinful, stubborn heart. (See 1 Samuel 15:23.) The difference between these two men is that David submitted his entire being to God, and Saul spent the majority of his latter years running from God's authority and living by his own authority.

Dreams and Destiny

Everybody has dreams; some we remember, some dreams we forget when we wake up. Sometimes our dreams are so bizarre we blame the Mexican food we had for dinner. God uses dreams to speak to His people. He uses them in several different ways; sometimes for warnings, sometimes for direction, like the one that I had when I was always running. In that particular recurrence, God was showing me that I was running from Him and the unresolved issues I had built up in my heart. He was trying to get my attention, but it took a long time for me to see His warnings and to face those issues.

Another type of dream that God will use to speak to us is what I refer to as destiny dreams. Many people have had ministry calls through dreams; calls to preach, evangelize, or go to the mission field. Some people have prophetic dreams about things to come, both good and bad. Sometimes God speaks to His people with dreams that need interpreting because they are symbolic in nature. This is how God spoke many times in the scriptures and even how He speaks today.

The story of Joseph is a good example of how God speaks to His people through dreams. In Genesis 30:24, we first hear about Joseph whose name means "may he add" or "increaser." He was the eleventh son of Jacob and Jacob's favorite son because he was the son of his old age. For that reason, Joseph's brothers were jealous and envious of him. In Genesis 37, Joseph, who was seventeen at the time, had two dreams, both of which were symbolic. Since symbolic dreams require interpretation, the Lord gave Joseph the understanding of the dreams. In essence, the dreams showed that one day Joseph's father, mother, and brothers would bow down to him. Joseph, being young and zealous, shared this dream with his family who also understood the meaning of the symbolism. His father, Jacob, became angry with Joseph and his brothers became even more upset with him. They were sure they would never bow down to their younger brother!

One day, Joseph's brothers were tending the flock in a distant city when Jacob sent Joseph to check on them. They saw him coming and conspired to kill him. In the end, they chose instead to sell him as a slave to passing merchants. As a cover-up, they killed a young goat and dipped Joseph's coat in its blood, tore it, and told their father Jacob that a wild animal had killed him. These merchants then sold Joseph in Egypt to Potiphar, an officer of Pharaoh and the captain and chief executioner of the guard. So now Joseph is a slave. To Joseph this certainly must have been confusing. God gave him this great dream, and the next thing that happens is he ends up a slave in a foreign country! Did God make a mistake? Of course not!

God was with Joseph and he found favor with Potiphar. Potiphar put him in charge of his entire household. (See Genesis 39.) One day Potiphar's wife tried to seduce Joseph. He resisted her advances but as he fled from the house, she grabbed his coat and used it to blackmail him, saying he tried to rape her. Potiphar then threw him in prison. Can you imagine how confused Joseph must have felt about all of this?

God was still with Joseph and he found favor with the prison warden who put him in charge of all the prisoners in the jail. (See Genesis 40.) One day Pharaoh became angry with his chief butler and baker and threw them into the same prison Joseph was in. Then one night, the butler and baker each had a dream. They told their dreams to Joseph, and God blessed him with the interpretation. When the dreams turned out the way Joseph had said, he told them not to forget him and to talk to Pharaoh about getting him out of prison. They forgot. Two years went by and Pharaoh had two dreams that nobody could interpret. (See Genesis 41.) Then the chief butler remembered Joseph in prison and told Pharaoh about his dream and Joseph's interpretation.

Pharaoh summoned Joseph who provided him with the correct interpretation of his dream. Pharaoh was so pleased with Joseph that he promoted him to second in charge of all the land of Egypt, changed his name, and gave him a wife. There was no one higher than Joseph except Pharaoh. Joseph was now thirty years old, and it had been thirteen years since he had the original dream. However, he never gave up on that dream and he held it in his heart.

The dreams Joseph interpreted for Pharaoh were warnings from God that there were going to be seven years of prosperity followed by seven years of famine. During those seven years of prosperity, much grain was stored up. When the famine hit, all the countries, including Israel, came to Joseph to buy grain. Are you beginning to see the picture here? Jacob heard about the grain in Egypt and sent ten of his sons to buy grain. It had now been twenty-two years since they had last seen Joseph, so when his brothers approached him, they didn't recognize him. (See Genesis 42.) But Joseph knew who they were. In Genesis 43 and 44, Joseph managed to get all his brothers to Egypt and then in Genesis 45, he revealed himself to them. After all those years of trials, Joseph did not hold any anger against his brothers. Then Pharaoh told Joseph's brothers to go get their father, all their family, cattle, and possessions, and he would give them some land.

In Genesis 45:8 (NRSV) Joseph said "It was not you who sent me here, but God." In Genesis 50:18–20 Joseph's brothers fell down before him saying that they were his servants. Joseph's reply was that what they had meant for evil against him, God had turned around for good so their lives would be spared when the famine came. That dream was so embedded in Joseph's spirit that it nearly became part of his DNA. Joseph did not know God's purposes for these trials, but he did know God's character and promises, and those are what sustained him. The dream belonged to God. From the birthing of the dream to the fulfillment of it, God's purposes needed to be accomplished in Joseph's life to develop the character he needed for the dream to come to pass.

God may have given you great dreams or desires; however, your character may not be able to support them at this time. God's timing is perfect, and He knows what you need and how you need to grow in order to fulfill them. It is imperative that we, as His children, allow God to grow and change us so that His perfect will may be accomplished in our lives. Don't fight your way through the trials you are facing, and don't get impatient. Pray for the strength to grow and endure trying times so that God's perfect will for your life will come to pass. Pray it into existence. Then trust God to do the rest, just as Joseph did.

God gave me a dream that I would be moving and He showed me what the street would look like as well as the interior surroundings. I did not know when God's timing would be for that dream to be fulfilled in my life but from that point on that dream was etched into my spirit. Over two years later that dream came to fruition, but during those two years, the Lord dealt with me about my fear, doubt, lack of faith and trust I had in Him. I am sure there was a lot more that God was doing in my life that I was not even aware of at the time.

Trusting God from the time He gave me the dream about moving until it was time to start packing boxes was a huge step of faith for me, but when the time came, I was ready and everything went smoothly. I had no doubt that my God was going to supply all my needs, and of course He did. But first He had to develop more of His character in me to take me where I needed to go. He even had to heal some of my wounds from the past that would have totally incapacitated me. He is a merciful God and He knows us better than we know ourselves. I have grown so much closer to Him because of the trials, the valleys, and the bumps in the road. I have had to die figuratively to my own desires for God to be able to work in me so deeply and fruitfully.

Death Comes Before Resurrection

No one has had a perfect childhood. You know the "Leave It to Beaver" kind of family; dad goes to work, mom stays home, the kids go to school, there is a white picket fence around the house, a dog in the backyard, a swing set, and a station wagon in the driveway. My dream for this type of family life died when I was six and my parents divorced. It was very hard to let that dream die, but things happen. People divorce. Sometimes they die.

Some people seemingly have these picture-perfect families. However, what you may not see is the lack of love or the emotional, physical, or verbal abuse. The term everyone is using today is "dysfunctional" and seems to be a good excuse for everything that goes wrong in our lives.

Here is an example: you are eighteen, have left

that "'dysfunctional" family, and started a life of your own. You vowed never to let that happen in your family. Therefore, the search begins for that "perfect" mate. You think you have found a suitable candidate so you marry and make big plans for your future together. Soon you have a house with a white picket fence, a dog in the backyard, and a baby. You even attend church every Sunday. All of the sudden your husband or wife has met someone "more suitable" and wants a divorce. Another dream dies.

You are the first string quarterback going to the Super Bowl next week, you trip over a toy at home and dislocate the shoulder on your throwing arm. No going to that Super Bowl. You are a skilled surgeon and have a car accident which leaves you with nerve damage in your arm and you can't hold a scalpel. Your child gets cancer at age six and dies. All these are examples of broken dreams. All bring emotional pain that is beyond comprehension. Instead of blaming God, which we all tend to do at times, realize that He *is* your strength to go on. He is your Comforter and Deliverer; an ever present help in time of trouble. (See Psalm 46:1.)

Nearly everyone has heard Psalm twenty-three at some point in their lives. This is a great psalm; one which can help us through our everyday trials. God says He will be with us when we walk *through* the valley. Do not stop in the valley and camp, keep going! There are many things we will never understand about God, but that does not mean we should trust Him less. He has a perfect plan for your life.

> For I know the thoughts and plans that I have
> for you, says the LORD, thoughts and plans for

The Desires of the Heart

welfare and peace and not for evil, to give you hope in your final outcome.
—JEREMIAH 29:11, AMP

Sometimes our desires are not God's desires. There have been times when I have pleaded with God for something and never received what I asked for. Then I found James 4:3 which says, "You do ask and yet fail to receive because you ask with wrong purpose and evil, selfish motives…to spend it in sensual pleasures." Ouch! That was exactly the problem. The desire was to make me look more important, or to keep up with the Joneses, or prove something to somebody, etc., etc. The focus was all about *me* and not about God or giving Him glory. Sometimes you have to throw your hands up in surrender and release the desires in your heart for things that are not of God. This is what the Bible calls "crucifying the flesh" in Galatians 5:24, "with its passions and appetites and desires."

Remember Abraham back in chapter three? I am sure Abraham had truly desired to have children. It was the custom in that day to have many children. Abraham had one wife, Sarah, and she was barren. But the desire was always there for both of them. Then God confirmed that desire by speaking a word to Abraham telling him he would be the father of a multitude. He was seventy-five at the time and Sarah was sixty-five. Twelve years went by and still no baby. Now Sarah decided to help God out and had the idea that Abraham, who was now eighty-six years old, should sleep with her servant girl, Hagar, as to have a baby with her. Sarah became impatient while waiting for God's promised child to be born to them. Hagar conceived and a baby boy named Ishmael was born. Ishmael was not the child God had in mind when He had originally spoken to Abraham.

Thirteen years later at age ninety-nine, God told Abraham that the child of His promise would come from his union with Sarah who was now eighty-nine. By now, Abraham and Sarah's dreams had to be totally dead. This is what God wanted, dead dreams and worn out bodies to show His glory and faithfulness to Israel. Out of this seemingly impossible situation, God can receive all the glory. In Genesis 18, Sarah conceived Isaac at age eighty-nine. This was a medical miracle!

The moral of the story is this: if you put your total focus on your dream or desire, God may require it of you in order to get your focus back on Him. He may ask you to give it up. I have had dreams that I had to let go of because I got so obsessed and frustrated trying to make them happen on my own. It takes a lot of work when you do it that way. But if your dream is truly from God and everything's in the proper alignment with the focus on God, *He* will make it happen in His way and in His time. You will be amazed at the ease in which things begin to flow when we give God control. His timing is always perfect. So why struggle? Give your dreams over to God. Let Him know that He is the desire of your heart. Let go of your idols; let *Him* resurrect them for you, in His time and in His excellent way. God has a wonderful plan for you. You may have to sacrifice what you think is good to get God's best. God says in Ephesians 3:20–21 (NIV), "Now to him who is able to do immeasurably more than all we ask or imagine, according to his power that is at work within us, to him be glory in the church and in Christ Jesus throughout all generations, for ever and ever! Amen." That is a promise, but do not forget the most important thing…put Him first in your life!

The Matter of the Heart

When we are born again, we give our hearts in surrender to God. Most of the references to the "heart" in the Old Testament refer to the Hebrew word *labe*, which means "the feelings, the will, and the intellect." In the New Testament the Greek word is *kardia*, meaning "the thoughts or feelings." At the time of salvation, God saves and converts your spirit or your "spiritual heart."

The Bible also clearly tells us that we must renew our minds with the Word of God. (See Ephesians 4:23.) By reading the Word of God and spending time in His presence, you begin to understand God, His views, and the way He thinks. You begin to see the world through His eyes, hate the things He hates, love the things He loves, know what hurts Him and what gives Him joy.

They played *Taps* at my Dad's military funeral. For years after that, every time I heard that song I would break down and cry because I would think of my dad and how much I missed him. My husband knew that about me, so when we had the TV on and they would begin to play that song, he would hit the mute button so I would not have to hear it. Eventually, the Lord healed that wound in my heart, and took the pain from those memories. Now it no longer affects me that way.

When God speaks to us, He speaks to our spiritual heart. However, if our mind has not been transformed by His Word, what we hear we will reject. That is because what the Lord speaks to our heart, usually doesn't make any sense to our mind. The mind and the heart are opposed to each other and are constantly fighting against each other. Our carnal nature is fighting with our spiritual nature or our mind against our heart. Unless you really get to know God and His ways, this will make you crazy!

Before my father passed away, I did everything possible to try to earn his love. I never felt like I did enough and constantly felt guilty. When I was born again, I felt the same way about my heavenly Father. I did a lot of religious works trying to earn God's approval that not only appeased my conscience, but that I hoped would impress others as well as God. But the guilt was still there and I never quite felt like I had done enough to be pleasing and acceptable to God, so I kept doing more. What I did not realize at the time was that I was in bondage.

Then I began to understand the righteousness of God.

> For our sake He made Christ to be sin who knew no sin, so that in and through Him we might become...the righteousness of God.
> —2 Corinthians 5:21, AMP

The great revelation I had was that when Jesus died on the cross for my sins, that was all it took. My debt to God for my sin was paid. I do not have to work for my salvation or to earn God's favor. My right standing with God is not based on my performance, but on my

The Desires of the Heart

faith and trust in Jesus Christ as my personal Savior and Lord. The blood of Jesus made it possible for me to be right with God. I may not do everything right but that does not change who I am or how God feels about me. God sees my heart and that I want to obey Him and be pleasing to Him. He is patient with my shortcomings and forgives me when I stumble.

What is the motive behind your actions? I would do things because I felt I had to and murmur and complain about them the entire time. This was a wrong heart motive. Jesus said I got my reward in full right then and there. (See Matthew 6:2.) I did not store up any eternal rewards because of the attitude of my heart. As a Christian you need to examine the motives behind your actions and make sure they line up with the mind and attitude of Christ.

When your renewed mind lines up with the conversion that has taken place in your spirit, you become a new creation, inside and out. The only way your renewed mind can fail to come into harmony with your new heart is by a choice of your own will. You must choose whether to follow the habits that are stored up in your memories or to submit them to the issues that flow from your heart. You can do it, but be patient with yourself. Remember, we are being changed from "glory to glory" or "good to better to best" over a period of time. (See 2 Corinthians 3:18.) There is rhythm to a heartbeat that we need to get in sync with.

The mysteries of our heart are fully known to God. Jeremiah 17:9-10 (NLT) says, "The human heart is most deceitful and desperately wicked. Who really knows how bad it is? But I know! I, the LORD, search all hearts and examine secret motives. I give all people their due rewards, according to what their actions deserve." You cannot hide anything from God. God says to obey is better than sacrifice. (See 1 Samuel 15:22.) The Bible says to draw near to God with a true heart, and He'll draw near to you and direct you. (See Hebrews 10:22.)

In 1 Samuel 13, King Saul did not obey the command of the Lord because his heart was wicked. So God replaced him with David whom God said "was a man after His own heart" (verse 14). But David was *far* from perfect.

Before David became king, he was a shepherd boy in his father's field and the youngest of eight sons. He was also the one to slay the giant Goliath. (See I Samuel 17.) It took many years for God to prepare David to become king. He was the armor bearer and played the harp for King Saul. He became best friends with King Saul's son Jonathan. After David killed Goliath, King Saul became jealous of David and set out to kill him. David had to flee for his life until one day, King Saul and Jonathan were both killed in battle. Though King Saul tried to kill him, David was extremely sorrowful in his heart about their deaths.

As the king of Israel, David accomplished many things because God was with him. But David, the man, made a lot of mistakes. It was forbidden in those days for a king to have more than one wife, but David had several. David also had an adulterous relationship with Bathsheba who became pregnant. David eventually killed her husband to cover his sin and then married her. The baby she bore died, but

David and Bathsheba conceived another child, Solomon, who eventually became king.

David was also a writer. He is responsible for writing 73 of the Psalms. David's Psalms are great hymns of praise to God, but they also put into words some of the most agonizing difficulties every believer faces. When the prophet Nathan confronted David about his sin with Bathsheba, he wrote Psalm 32 and Psalm 51, confessing his sin and rejoicing over God's forgiveness. In Psalm 51:10, David asks God to "create in me a clean heart, O God, and renew a right, persevering, and steadfast spirit within me" (RSV). This should be our prayer as well. The Bible says that we must have clean hands and a pure heart; without which no one can see God. (See Psalm 24.) Jesus also says in Matthew 5:8, "Blessed are the pure in heart, for they will see God" (NIV).

Going through the process of purification can be rough, but God will help you. When your heart has been made pure by the Spirit of the Lord; you come into a place that aligns you with God's will and desires for your life. Your heart starts to crave the things of God. His desires become your desires.

> The kingdom of God is not a matter of food and drink, but instead it is righteousness and peace and joy in the Holy Spirit.
> —ROMANS 14:17, AMP

After God had cleaned out my heart, I noticed that those things that I thought I absolutely had to have to survive in life did not really matter anymore. My whole outlook had changed. My needs and desires had changed for the better. I still enjoy a nice house, a nice car, nice clothes, and peace in my relationships. But there was a new freedom in my life that I had never experienced before. I never realized how deep the bondage really was. Though I am far from perfect and make a lot of mistakes, I know my heart is bent toward God. He is gentle as He works with me and changes me. I have never known such peace and such freedom. God is no respecter of persons; you can have that too. (See Acts 10:34.)

Be Anxious for Nothing

> Be anxious for nothing, but in everything by prayer and supplication with thanksgiving let your requests be made know to God. And the peace of God, which surpasses all comprehension, will guard your hearts and your minds in Christ Jesus.
>
> —PHILIPPIANS 4:6–7, NASB

Peace is a word many of us know very little about. Our natural, carnal way of handling circumstances is to have anxiety, confusion, fear, and stress. A normal day in my life used to encompass all of those emotions! I used to say that I worked best under pressure. I am your typical Type A, or choleric, personality; a planner, a goal setter, and very determined, hard headed and stubborn. I would undertake a project, plan it in my mind, then go at it until it was finished, usually quicker than thought humanly possible. I drove fast, ate fast, cleaned the house fast. Everything I did was fast. I loved activity and was always busy. But I had no peace.

I had a lot of pride and independence in my life, both of which were sin for me. It is not wrong to be independent in itself, but for me, I realized that independence displays a lack of trust in God. Over the years, God has been at work in my life. I am no longer as independent, but God-dependent. I have learned through experience that if I had just asked God, I would have avoided much pain, expense, and aggravation. I still make mistakes and do not always pray things through. Sometimes I rush out ahead of God or miss Him altogether. But if I miss Him, He still finds me and helps me make the best of the situation when I come back to Him. (See Romans 8:28.) I am a living example of a life changed solely by God over time and for the better. I found that place of peace and rest and will not let anything take the peace of God away from me. Once you have tasted it, you will not want to let go of it either.

> A man's mind plans his way, but the LORD directs his steps.
> —PROVERBS 16:9, RSV

The Lord wants us to use our minds and the wisdom He has given us. He allows us to make decisions but will sometimes restrain us or make us feel uneasy in our spirit if we are going in a wrong direction or heading for trouble. This is what some call a check in your spirit or getting a red flag.

> The steps of a man are directed and established by the LORD.
> —PSALM 37:23

When we are submitted to the Lord and admit our dependence on Him, He will direct our path. He will show us how to attain that which we are in need of.

You will be able to attune yourself to His leading and directions.

When the Lord told me He wanted me to move to California, I was in a state of shock. God's plans often surprised us, and this definitely was a surprise. Everything was going smoothly in my life up to that point. Then that carnal nature, otherwise known as panic, kicked in. I had a tremendous amount of things I had to take care of; sell the condo, sell the business, get a job, find a place to live. The list went on. I didn't know where to go from that point. Fear set in and peace went out the door.

I fasted and prayed, asking God to confirm His will and His word to me. He kept bringing me back to Abraham who left his country to a place God would show him. Somebody gave me a tape that listed seven people in the Bible who up and moved based on a word from the Lord. Over and over again, the Lord gave me confirmations from preachers I saw on TV, something I would read, or scriptures from my quiet times. I was still was not sure of which direction to take and kept trying to figure it all out. The only thing I did not get from God that I was hoping for was an email!

I went through this for five months. Then one day I was out of town at a meeting, and a minister was talking about sowing a *radical* financial seed against a urgent need you had. I do sow seeds of faith and pray over every tithe and offering check. But I felt impressed that the Lord was telling me to pledge $1,000. I didn't have that kind of money and had no idea of where I would get it, but I was obedient and pledged that $1,000, which God did provide supernaturally in the next thirty days. When I returned home, I prayed a prayer that my mind heard as my mouth spoke it. I told the Lord that I just was not going to worry about this anymore. He already knew the timing of the move, the place I would live, and the job I would hold. I surrendered all responsibility of making this happen. It was now His job to bring it to pass. There was such faith in that prayer that I surprised myself. From that time forward, I had entered what I now know as the "rest of God." No more striving, no more fear, no more worry, no more struggle; just perfect peace.

Hebrews chapter four also talks about God's promise of rest. Verse 10 says, "For all who enter into God's rest will find rest from their labors, just as God rested after creating the world."(NLT) To enter that rest is not to be inactive or lazy but to be free and joyful in your service to God, not being weighed down with all those things listed above. In Matthew 11:28 Jesus says, "Come to me, all you who labor and are heavy laden and overburdened, and I will cause you to rest." That is exactly what Jesus did for me. He relieved my burden.

When it came time, I was willing to make the move because I knew God had a plan for me there and I was eager to find out what it was. Now my attitude was like the old song said, "what will be will be." I listed the condo and I knew it would not sell a minute before the right time. I knew the job would show up right on time. I even had perfect peace when I got there which happened to be eighteen months after the Lord had first spoke it to me. I knew that God had truly made this happen and I did not have anything to do with it. The town, the apartment, everything was perfect. Best of all, all these things truly were the hidden desires of my heart.

In Luke 12:22–34, Jesus was talking with His disciples about anxiety.

> Look at the lilies and how they grow. They don't work or make their clothing, yet Solomon in all his glory was not dressed as beautifully as they are. And if God cares so wonderfully for flowers that are here today and gone tomorrow, won't he more surely care for you? You have so little faith. And don't worry about food—what to eat and drink. Don't worry whether God will provide it for you. These things dominate the thoughts of most people, but your Father already knows your needs. He will give you all you need from day to day if you make the kingdom of God your primary concern.
> —LUKE 12:27–31, NLT

That is a wonderful promise from our Lord if we will put Him first in our lives. Once the Holy Spirit got this deep down in my spirit, I entered that place of rest. I had such peace and comfort knowing my loving, heavenly Father would take care of my every need and desire.

Verse 34 of that chapter says, "For where your treasure is, there will your heart be also" (NIV). Once God becomes your treasure, He becomes your heart's desire. When He becomes your heart's desire, the blessings of heaven belong to you. Give yourself completely to God, trust Him, and He will give Himself to you. Take that leap of faith!

CHAPTER FIVE

GIVE AND IT SHALL BE GIVEN

When we surrender our lives to the lordship of Jesus Christ, we are not giving but getting. We give Him all that we are in exchange for all that He is. Wow, that is far from an even exchange! In this final chapter, I want to discuss some of the things that Jesus died to give us.

God Had Another Plan

Jesus Christ is the ultimate gift of God to a doomed human race. Due to Adam and Eve's sin, we, being their descendants, were eternally separated from God. God had a wonderful plan for us; daily walks in the garden with Him, talking with Him face to face. Before the fall of man there was no disease, pain in childbirth, fighting, death, or any other kind of evil in the world. Man's rebellion disrupted God's plan for mankind in the garden of Eden. At one point, God was sorry He had even made man. (See Genesis 6:6–7.)

God had another plan. He gave the life of His Son, Jesus, in exchange for ours so that mankind could be reunited with their Creator. Through the shed blood of Jesus, we can again have access to God the Father. Jesus is, in essence, our "bridge" to God.

> So it is written, "The first Adam became a living being. The last Adam [Christ] became a life-giving Spirit.
> —1 CORINTHIANS 15:45, NKJV

We were dead spiritually because of Adam and destined to spend eternity in hell, but Jesus came to redeem us and restore us to life. God bought us back with the blood of His Son Jesus.

Leviticus 17:11 (KJV) says, "For the life of the flesh is in the blood." We all know how important our blood is to our physical bodies. It carries life-giving oxygen and food throughout our system, as well as acting as a defense against infection. Our bodies cannot live without blood. We may never fully understand the value that God places on the blood of Jesus. Why His blood? Because life is in the blood, and life is the only antidote for death. If you drank poison, you would need to get the proper antidote in order to live. Jesus' shed blood is the proper antidote for the poison of sin that came to us through the bloodline of Adam.

> For our sake He made Christ to be sin who knew no sin, so that in and through Him we might become the righteousness of God.
> —2 CORINTHIANS 5:21

God *gave* His Son as a sacrifice for us. We will never fully be able to comprehend the incredible love God has for us in order to do that.

When I first was saved, I knew I would go to heaven because I believed in Jesus and His sacrificial death. But there is so much more to redemption than that. If I had only known that in the beginning, I would have had a better chance of not falling away from God for those awful seventeen years. God gave Adam authority on the earth. Through his sin, Adam gave that authority to Satan. Through the death of Jesus and His shed blood, we, as believers, now take that authority back from Satan. God wants us to live in victory rather than in defeat. God has already made all the arrangements, and has prepared the way for us. We just need to learn how to walk in that authority. God has raised us up and seated us in heavenly places, high places, not low places. (See Ephesians 2:5–6.) We are the head and not the tail, above and not beneath. (See Deuteronomy 28:13.)

The devil would like to keep us broke, busted, and disgusted. But we have authority over him and we need to learn to use that authority. Jesus says in John 10:10, "The thief [Satan] comes only in order to steal and kill and destroy. I [Jesus] came that they may have and enjoy life, and have it in abundance."

Before we can understand all that Christ died to give us, we have to understand who we are in Christ by understanding who He is. This is made clear through the names He is given in the Bible.

There Is Power in the Name of Jesus

> That in the name of Jesus every knee should bow, in heaven and on earth and under the earth.
> —PHILIPPIANS 2:10, NIV

We have learned some of the names of the Holy Spirit and of God the Father. But the name of *Jesus* is the highest and most powerful name of all. I pray right now that the Holy Spirit gives you revelation about the name of Jesus and the power it holds for every believer.

When a couple gets married, the wife takes on the husband's surname. She now has the power of attorney to use her husband's name. Each other's personal possessions now become joint, but only after the marriage, not before. That is how it is when we are born again. We take on the name of Jesus and now become identified with Him. We have the legal right to use His name. The Bible says Jesus is the bridegroom and we are the bride of Christ. (See John 3:29.)

Peter used God's authority or the name of Jesus in Acts 3:1–7. Peter and John were going to the temple one day when they came across a man who was crippled from birth and who was brought to the gate of the temple every day begging for gifts. Peter said to him in verse 6, "Silver and gold I do not have; but what I do have, that I give to you: in the name of Jesus Christ of Nazareth, walk!" Then they took him by the hand, stood him up, and his legs and ankles became strong. He went leaping and dancing and praising God all the way down the street. Peter and John had a revelation of the power in the name of

Give and It Shall Be Given

Jesus that was available to them and they used it.

The name of Jesus also gives us His authority. In Luke 9:1–2, Jesus gave his disciples (and us as well) power and authority over all demons. We can pray for the sick and they will recover when we pray with faith in the name of Jesus. (See James 5:15–16.)

Joyce Meyer tells a story of a friend who was driving down the road with his three- or four-year-old son in the passenger seat of the car.[1] He did not realize that the passenger side door was not securely shut so when he made a sharp turn, his son flew out of the car and into the middle of traffic at a busy intersection (this was before the seat belt laws were passed). The last thing the father saw was a set of car wheels just about to run over his son. All he knew to do was to cry, "Jesus." He stopped the car and ran to his son, who just had a few scratches. The man who almost hit the little boy was hysterical. As the father tried to comfort the man and tell him it was OK and how glad he was that he was able to stop in time, the driver said, "You don't understand, I never touched my brakes." The power in the name of Jesus saved that boy's life.

Jesus says in John 14:14 (KJV), "If ye shall ask anything in my name, I will do it." The name of Jesus is not some type of a magical word we can use at will to get what we want. We must be walking in obedience to the Lord and ask according to His will. How can we know His will if we do not know Him? By reading His Word and spending time in His presence. John 15:7 (KJV) says, "If ye abide in me, and my words abide in you, ye shall ask what ye will, and it shall be done unto you." To *abide* means "to remain, to stay closely connected, to settle in for the long term." It requires an action. Once we begin to know Him through His Word, we begin to understand Him and His will. When our will lines up with His will, then we can ask what we want in the name of Jesus and He will do it because we are asking in faith according to His will.

Are you beginning to see and understand the power that is in the name of Jesus? There are over 700 biblical names, titles, symbols, similes, descriptions, and designations used in reference to Jesus in the Bible. Each one depicts some aspect of Jesus' character. Here are a few of my favorites. Read down the list slowly and let them sink deep down into your spirit.

- The Beginning and the End (Revelation 21:6)
- The Bread of Life (John 6:35)
- Eternal Life (1 John 5:20)
- Faithful and True (Revelations 19:11)
- High Priest (Hebrews 4:14)
- Our Hope (1 Timothy 1:1)
- Husband (2 Corinthians 11:2)
- The Image of God (2 Corinthians 4:4)
- The King of Kings (1 Timothy 6:15)
- The Lamb of God (John 1:36)
- The Light of the World (John 9:5)
- The Lord of All (Romans 10:12)
- The Lord, Your Redeemer (Isaiah 43:14)

- The Only Begotten Son (John 1:18)
- The Physician (Luke 4:23)
- The Prince of Peace (Isaiah 9:6)
- The Same, Yesterday, Today and Forever (Hebrews 13:8)
- The Resurrection and the Life (John 11:25)
- Savior (1 Timothy 4:10)
- The Way, the Truth, and the Life (John 14:6)
- The Word of Life (1 John 1:1)

There are still so many other wonderful names. Each one reveals His character, who He is to us, and what He has done for us. We will never fully be able to grasp all the power that is behind that name. The devil hates the name of Jesus because he knows he has to bow to it. Use the name of Jesus against the enemy, when you pray for others and in adoration and thanksgiving.

Jesus...there is something about that wonderful name. Jesus came not only to redeem us from sin and give us eternal life, but to give us a better life.

Abundant Life

Jesus said in John 10:10 (NIV), "The thief [Satan] comes only to steal and kill and destroy; I have come that they may have life, and have it to the full." We are children of the Most High God! God did not intend for us to live broken and defeated lives. We just need to learn how to obtain that physical, spiritual, financial, and emotional freedom that is available to us.

Luke 2:40 (NKJV) talks about Jesus as a child who "grew and became strong in spirit, filled with wisdom; and the grace of God was upon Him." Everything we need to be happy, healthy, prosperous, and successful in our Christian walk is in this verse. We think we need "things" but what we really need is to become strong in spirit, filled with God's wisdom, and having His grace upon us. Grace means unmerited favor. We do not deserve it, but God freely gives it because we are in a covenant or a relationship with Him.

When we mature spiritually and grow in God's wisdom and grace, we will begin to really believe that God is in complete control of our life and to trust Him in all things. Through it all, we will know that God is working out His plan for us. We may not always get everything we want, but we *will* have *everything* we need. (See Matthew 6:33.) You may not get it when you want it, but God's timing is perfect. He knows what is best for you because He knows you better than you will ever know yourself. He also knows that if He gave you all of the things you really think you want, they would probably destroy you.

Paul tells us in Ephesians 2:10 (AMP), "For we are God's handiwork, recreated in Christ Jesus, that we may do those good works which God predestined for us, that we should walk in them." It is great to have goals, plans, and dreams for your life—things you are believing God for. Habakkuk 2:2 tells us to write our visions and dreams and to visualize them. If you have had those plans for a long time but you do not seem to be getting any closer to achieving them, maybe its time to put those dreams aside. There may be something better God has planned for you but your eyes have been blinded to it because you are focusing on your own desires rather than listening to God. Lay it down for a moment.

God's time is not the same as our human interpretation of it. God knows the exact time when we need things. I had a dream one time that I knew was from God. I was single and living alone at the time and so was my mom. I knew the Lord wanted us to sell our respective homes and live together. That was a hard word for me because my mom and I are both very strong-willed, independent women who like our space.

There was no apparent reason why God would have us move in together. We were both secretly hoping this was just a test to see if we were willing. Nevertheless, I was sure that God had a good reason for it and He would give us the grace we needed. We found a place large enough to provide us each with a reasonable amount of personal space, so I put my condo up for sale. I knew that God was in this and felt that the condo would sell quickly. However, after several months of no offers, I remembered that I never asked God about His timing. With my condo looking as if it were not going to sell in the near future, I decided that God was telling me it was not the right time yet, so I put the plans for my mother and I to live together on hold. Two and a half years later, it was finally time. During those couple of years, God did some deep healing in my life of emotional wounds from my childhood. We would have literally killed each other if we had moved in when *I* thought we were supposed to with the emotional baggage I was still carrying around inside of me. Thank God for His perfect timing. I learned an important lesson in patience from that experience. The only way to develop patience in life is to go through experiences that require you to be patient. Nobody likes them, but everybody needs them.

The moral of this story is: God had given me His plan, but time and healing were necessary for both of us in order for that plan to succeed. Not only was there emotional healing between my mother and myself during that time, but the value of both of our homes skyrocketed during that two year period. God was taking care of us in way we never would have imagined.

God desires to provide for our financial needs as well as our spiritual needs. But there are principles in the Bible that we must follow. This principle is most often referred to as sowing and reaping. Galatians 6:7 says, "For whatever a man sows, this he will also reap" (NASB). I have learned this to be true in *all* things in life, not only financial things. When I sow words of encouragement in someone's life, then when I need encouragement, God sends someone to encourage me. When I cut someone off in traffic, I get cut off shortly thereafter. If I eat a diet high in saturated fat, then I run the risk of developing heart disease. If I cheat someone, I lose money.

Malachi 3:10 (NIV) says, "Bring all the tithes into the storehouse, that there may be food in My house, and prove Me now by it, says the LORD of hosts, if I will not open the windows of heaven for you and

Give and It Shall Be Given

pour you out a blessing, that there shall not be room enough to receive it." The first check I write out from every paycheck is my tithe check. Ten percent (of the gross) goes to my church. I also send out offerings in addition to one or two other ministries that feed me spiritually and I feel the Lord drawing me to. Year after year I gave faithfully and I still felt like I was just getting by on my paycheck. I knew God's promises were true, but I didn't feel like I was getting ahead monetarily. One day, I realized that I was getting by on my paycheck. There was nothing lacking in my life. I realized that my twelve-year-old appliances never broke down; my clothes didn't wear out, my fourteen-year-old car never broke down; I was healthy; my cats were healthy; I had peace and joy in my life. I may not have been reaping a large monetary profit in a bank account, but I was receiving many financial and spiritual blessings from God in other ways.

I was faithful in my giving even when it was hard and I was discouraged. God says He loves a cheerful giver. (See 2 Corinthians 9:7.) I changed my attitude. An evangelist once said that he and his wife would lay their hands on their check and aim it at a need they had. I started to do that with all my needs, after all God said to "prove Him." He always met my needs, right on time, of course, and sometimes not always in the way I expected.

After years of faithfully sowing and from time to time aiming that seed at financial freedom, the day came when I was able to sell my condo. My years of prayers were wonderfully answered and every one of my bills were paid off and money left over. Only by the grace of God could that happen. All glory belongs to God, because if I had not waited on God's timing, I would have made a mess of the whole thing and missed what He was trying to provide for me.

Be patient. Trust God that He will answer your prayers in accordance to His timing and will. He will always answer. He knows what you need even before you ask (See Matthew 6:8.) If we try to make things happen on our own, we will have to maintain them on our own. But if we let God make things happen, He will take care of the details.

Let Go and Let God

God wants to change us from the inside out. He desires to give you peace and wholeness in your spirit, soul, and body. He wants to remove those things that keep tripping you up; heal those deep wounds you carry from the past, take away your fears, heal your body, and give you hope. Through the atonement of Jesus, we can have all these things and so much more. They have been bought and paid for with the blood of Jesus.

A few years after I had walked away from God, I left Illinois and moved to Florida. I was running from my past, hoping that all of the skeletons in my closet would stay in Illinois. But they did not. That baggage from the past moved to Florida with me.

During the seventeen years I ran from God, I went from being a workaholic, to an alcoholic, to struggling with codependency, and was just about to become fully engulfed in drug addiction when God rescued me; all of this in an attempt to suppress the pain that I lived with.

Most people did not really know what I was going through because I had this fake "happy face" I would wear. Inside, I was dying. After the Lord rescued me and I recommitted my life to Him, the destructive behavior stopped. He helped me clean my life up and removed a lot of the crud that had been weighing my spirit down. However, there was still a lot of baggage left. God led me to a great, loving, Spirit-filled church in Florida. I began to volunteer in the church office in my spare time and became friends with the pastor's wife, Ann, who was also an ordained minister. Soon after that, the Lord began to show me things. One day, He took me back to when I was eleven or twelve years old and an incident that happened to me. I asked Ann to pray for me because this had really upset me, just as it did back when I was a child. What happened next forever changed the course of my life...Ann and I went into her office where she asked me to close my eyes and picture that scene again. She asked me if I saw Jesus in that scene, and I did, standing right by the door. (I had not seen Him when I was a child.) Suddenly, peace washed over that scene and the anxiety disappeared. Just knowing that Jesus was there all the time brought healing to that memory. I was then able to forgive those involved and I was completely set free. The memory of those things did not go away, just the emotion and pain associated with it. It was as if the Lord edited that tape and erased the pain.

Regularly over the next five years, the Lord would show me things from my past that needed to be dealt with; pain that needed to be removed, hidden anger I was holding on to, people I needed to forgive. This wonderful woman of God, who will always be my best friend, gave me the tools I needed through Jesus Christ to get free from the issues of the past. I quickly learned how to deal with these memories and pull down the resulting strongholds they produced. God began to use my hurt and pain to help other people get free from their hurt and pain by placing me in an inner healing/prayer counseling ministry.

There were many times I did not want to revisit those places in my life God was touching on because they were too sensitive. There was one thing I just decided to hang on to because I was not ready to let go yet, it still hurt too much. But God kept gently nudging me to let it go and let Him bring healing. One Sunday Pastor Larry said that God will bring you to a place where the pain of remaining the same will exceed the pain of change. It seemed like he was talking right to me. I knew that was where I was, but this time I needed to have Ann's help and support. She had all the essentials ready, the Bible and a box of Kleenex. I felt like somebody had ripped my heart out. I went home and cried and slept then cried some more. But the next day, I had such peace and was kicking myself for not letting go sooner!

God is so faithful. He does not want us to live in bondage. Jesus came to give us abundant life, not just a daily existence. Jesus said in Luke 4:18–19, "The Spirit of the Lord is on me, because He has anointed me to preach the good news to the poor; He has sent me to announce release to the captives and recovery of sight to the blind, to send forth as delivered those who are oppressed to proclaim the accepted and acceptable year of the Lord." That is what He came for, to set us captives free! But in order to get free, we must surrender to Him, totally, completely. We must trust Him with every part of our lives, even those painful things.

Jesus says in Matthew 11:28 (KJV), "Come unto me all ye that labor, and are heavy laden, and I will give you rest." Your soul is made up of your mind, will, and emotions. That is where most of our unrest comes from. This step requires an action; "come unto me." It has to be a choice of your will. The Lord will never force you; He is gentle, and He is waiting for you to decide.

Once I had this first taste of freedom, I had no trouble giving God my fear, rejection, anger, guilt, shame, pride, bitterness, resentment—all of it. I gave him my broken dreams; I let Him heal those memories as He brought them to mind. I could write an entire book on the things God has delivered me from and is still freeing me from. Sanctification is an ongoing process. God knows the perfect time to bring things up and He never gives us more to deal with than we can bear. Since it took us years to get where we are, it will take some time to undo the damage we have acquired. It is like peeling an artichoke, one layer at a time until you get to the tender heart in the middle. The journey is important, including the little victories and the growth that comes from them.

In my life, I built a huge wall around myself to protect me from getting hurt. Because of that, I became a captive. That wall was so big and thick and high that for a very long time I would not even let God Himself in. It took years of breaking that wall down, brick by brick, before I was able to trust God not to hurt me. I just could not let go of my fear enough to let go and trust God. Then one day, I decided I was going to trust God. I got out the box of Kleenex, sat down on the floor (which is where I liked to pray), and did something that even surprised me. I offered my heart to God. It took a leap of faith for me to choose to trust God with my heart. I was terrified when I did it. The first few tests were tough, but now I have no fear that what the Lord tells me to do is the right thing. I obey without question and know He has my best interests in mind. How freeing that is! I know that no matter what happens in my life, good or bad, God will never let me get hurt again in any way that He cannot restore my heart and heal my spirit. I have learned that everything is for my benefit because there is a purpose behind each experience that God takes us through. Are you ready to let go and let God take over your life and your heart? This is my deepest desire for you! Above all, it is God's deepest desire for you.

---

1 Joyce Meyer, *The Word, the Name, the Blood* (Tulsa, OK: Harrison House, 1995).

Conclusion

God is on your side. He wants you to have a deep, fulfilling, fruitful life. Jesus died so that we could live eternally and have a relationship with our Creator. Our part is to make a choice to accept that sacrifice and live the life God has mapped out for us. There is nothing too awful that you have done in the past that God is unable to forgive and forget. Nothing! There is no pain or wound that He is unable to heal or deliver you from! There is no fear He is not willing to take away from you! The sacrifice has already been made. Now is the time to claim the promises of God!

If this book has caused you to hunger for the more of God and His righteousness, pray this prayer with me:

> *Dear heavenly Father,*
> *I accept the sacrifice that Jesus has made for me by dying on the cross for my sin, that I may live eternally with Him in heaven. I repent of my sins and choose to turn from my sinful ways. Come into my life, change me, set me free. I surrender to you the best I know how. I want to live the life you have planned for me. I want to know you more, Father, Son, and Holy Spirit. Fill me with Your Holy Spirit. Make all things new and fresh. I desire all that Jesus died for me to have. Strengthen me, direct my steps, renew my mind.*
> *Thank You, Father,*
> *In Jesus' name I pray, amen.*

Be sure to read your Bible everyday, even if only a chapter or two, beginning in the New Testament. Get a translation you can easily understand. Seek out a Spirit-filled church where you can grow in the things of God. Be sure to go every Sunday. Talk to the Lord every day, just tell Him what is on your heart. You are now on a wonderful new path. Be blessed as you go.

About the Author

Raeann Fitz has been a successful entrepreneur and owner of two service businesses. She was born in the suburbs of Chicago and now resides in Southern California. Her deepest desire is to help other Christians understand and walk in the fullness of life that is available to them. Through lessons learned from her life experiences, she wants to provide others with the tools they need to live a victorious Christian life.